for an okay free woman

poems by Lester Paldy

Night Heron Press

ISBN 0-9632277-0-X

Library of Congress Catalog Card Number 92-80282

Published by Night Heron Press
20 Night Heron Drive, Stony Brook, NY 11790

Printed at The Geryon Press, Limited, in Tunnel, New York

To my mother, Cele Gubernick Paldy

Contents

Where beach roses bloom

Whether the stars make any difference

Shoreward, toward home

No second chance

. . . where beach roses bloom

Morning Quartet

A dawn mist
covers the salt creek
and mud flats,
with the silence broken
only by gull cries,
the splash of baitfish,
and the muted sound
of oars.
The two swans
and dusky cygnet
seek bread,
wakes trailing behind.

When I first rowed
on this salt creek
the swans were wary,
but now they
let me approach
and we share
the solitude,
my sounds
counterpoint
to other rhythms
only they can hear.

Other World

The morning twilight
is just beginning
to warm the salt marsh
and shore where only
a few beach roses bloom now.
The sand in the shallows
is soft under my feet.
Killifish scatter
and a blue heron
springs into flight,
calling loudly against
the morning stillness.
As I swim from the shadows
into the sunlight,
my hands spray droplets
that shine
like diamonds and
fall back against
the calm surface.
A gull wheels above,
its head swiveling,
watching with unblinking eyes.
Now I am conscious only
of the water's touch
the taste of salt,
and the changing light.

Intuitions

Cold rain sweeps
the salt marsh
on this slate
dawn, pelting the reeds
and shrouding
the coast in mist.
The swans and cygnet
drift on the incoming tide,
hoping for bread,
trailing the oarsman who,
like the swans,
is silent,
borne on currents
he cannot know,
for while he sees
his wake bubbling
behind him,
he can only
try to sense
what lies beyond
the bend in the salt creek
where it turns
outward toward
the open sea.

Signs

A cold October wind
drives breakers
across the bay
in serried ranks.
Eatons Neck floats
on haze and the sunrise
tints a herring gull
gold against the sky.

The three swans sleep
in the marsh grass,
with necks arched backwards
and heads under their wings.
The cygnet has a few
white feathers
in its dusky tail.

Perhaps the swans
sense winter's nearness,
but they may only know
that the tide
rises and falls,
that day follows night,
leaving it for us
to interpret signs.

Changes

The cirrus-streaked cygnet
glides suspended
between water
and sky
arching its neck
as it preens.
There are hints
of more alchemy to come
in the markings
that shadow its eyes,
like those of a masked dancer
responding to a partner
yet unknown.

As the days grow shorter,
black ducks cluster near the reeds,
exploding into flight
with wing beats drumming
against the silence.
But the cygnet
is unafraid
and comes for bread
when I whistle,
its slow transformation
mirroring mine,
here where the marsh
marks the boundary
between the land
and restless sea.

Intrusion

Today a crowd of snails
greets me at the water's edge,
gently exploring
my intruding feet.
Hermit crabs admonish me,
ducking into their holes
and letting me know
whose beach it is.
When I pause
they wave their claws
but I don't respond.
They wait for
sexier crabs.

The blue heron
springs into the air
with a great
flapping of wings,
and raucous cries.
It is beautiful
in its wildness
and haughty disdain
for my company,
telling me
to expect no territorial
compromise from
the monarch of the marsh.

Flow

The flood tide
edges through
the marsh at dusk,
flowing quietly,
covering the grasses
with a silver palette
reflecting
a pastel sky.
The reeds sway
and mussels
along the bank
open, holding fast
to keep from
being swept away.
Time is short
and the tide
will ebb.
Glide in deep channels
while you may.

Markers

The storm tide
has swept away
the edge of the dune,
leaving behind
reeds and driftwood.
Now I carry stones
to the water's edge
to build a wall,
imagining how
drifting sand
will fill in gaps.
While I rest,
two swans fly
across the marsh,
their wing beats
like sighs
in the wind.
A stranded whelk
sits helpless
above the tide mark,
its parched foot
protruding from its shell.
When I return it
to the water,
it is still at first
but then it begins
digging slowly
into the sand.

The whelk and I
work at the edge
of the sea,
pitting muscle
and skill against
wind and tide.
We are patient,
measuring progress
in stones
and grains of sand.
The sea takes
our measure
as we work
to its rhythms,
framed by black pines
against the November sky.

Auguries

The surf murmur
lulls the marsh at dusk
and the sun sets
far to the southwest.
Low clouds drift
along the horizon
and marsh grasses
sway in the wind.
The creek is metallic
by twilight,
roiled by gusts
sweeping across
the barrier beach.
The moon tide courses
through the inlet,
pressing the bank
and spreading over
the salt meadow.
Far to the west
on a distant headland,
Eaton's Neck light
marks a safe harbor.
Across the sound,
mainland lights
stretch north.
Soon the first stars
shine on the marsh
whose changes
only hint at
the winter
yet to come.

Loons

The loons returned
to the salt creek today
riding a fresh
gale that carries whitecaps
across the Sound.
Now they dive for fish,
silhouetted darkly
against the water
and horizon.

There is something
different about loons.
Perhaps their wildness
reminds us that we do not
command the earth,
of depths we cannot plumb,
and insights
we can never have.
They course below
the mirrored surface
until they rise
in unexpected places
to startle us with
unblinking glances
that say their genomes,
more than ours,
match the marsh's patterns
of sand, water,
and reflected light.

Seawall

The stones just begin
to cover the dune's base now,
protecting it
from storm tides.
Working at the water's edge,
I thought of how
my father cleared trees
and built a wall
on a hillside long ago.
He was younger
than I am now
and I remember
his pull on the bucksaw.
Now my sons help
build a wall
we will finish by
the new moon.
Someday, when they sense
the memories
stored in the stones,
or steady a child
who teeters here
they may remember
how we built a wall
on the dune
where the beach roses
always bloom in summer.

Blue Heron

The heron
stood motionless
in the ebbing tide
and amber twilight,
as if waiting
for Hiroshige.
Then, striking fast,
it caught a fish.
If I could
concentrate
like that
I could do anything.

. . . whether the stars make any difference

If My Letters and Poems...

If my letters and poems
filed in corners
and odd places
slipped from their envelopes
shed their creases
and rustled and shook
their inked sheets
and became swans
they would spread their wings
and paddle furiously
with their hearts
beating fast
until with one great surge
they became creatures
of the air
flying free
over the marsh
with their calls
and wing sounds
like the words
there to remind you
whenever you heard
them of the infinite
varieties of love.

Atlantic Flight

Windborne now,
we slip away
to other lives,
I drawn by
the marsh and tides,
you to a great city.
Passing through
high cirrus
the plane trembles
miles above
waves that
break white
and then vanish.
Far below, petrels
skim over crests,
catching the light
with black-tipped wings,
their cries piercing
the hiss and tumult of
salt-spray,
reassurance
that they are
not alone
over the cold
and windswept sea.

for an okay free woman

the way it is
with you and me
is driving around
talking blue streaks
with the radio turned down
the way it is
after a thousand
goodbyes
and night landings
with strobe lights flashing
on runway markers
the way it is
when you put on
lipstick and say
you look awful
in daylight
while I think
you look beautiful
the way it is
when you tilt
your head back
and look at me
and I know you are
an okay free woman
ready to fly
like a bird
from the back
of my open hand
pointing exactly
to wherever
you want to go

Chamonix

If I were the man
and you were
the woman
we might drift
on this freshet
winding through
alpine meadows
brushed with lupine
until the water
sensed the land
falling away
beneath us
and spun us into
an inner space
of deep pools
and water lilies,
leaving us suspended
and alone,
with nothing
but ourselves
and what we know.

Anniversary Coincidence

How remarkable
that you
are so like
a girl
I loved
long ago
but perhaps
I sometimes
remind you
of a young man
you once knew
who told you
under crystal stars
that he would
love you
forever.

Bird on a Russian Pin

I don't mind
that you are
free in the wind
though I wish sometimes
you would
zoom down
perch on my shoulder
and trill
but I know you
must watch for snares
and will only
pause briefly
eyes bright and wary
before leaving
with just
a swaying branch
and downy feather
floating in the air
to remind me
that you are
much more
than an electric
flight of my
imagination.

FAX from Moscow Station

Hey lady a world away
in your housecoat
fine lines showing
your hair mussed
humming some song
legs drawn
beneath you
like a resting colt
reading a magazine
before you plan
for tomorrow
while seven time zones east
in a dingy hotel
Tsvetayeva's poems
glow like embers
in the cold
Russian night
but hey lady
in another world
all I really want
to say to you
tonight
is that the way
you are right now
mussed up hair
no make-up
whatever
would look
absolutely wonderful
to me.

Tiburon

We crossed the bay
on a sun-washed morning
watching the city
recede in the ferry's wake
as whitecaps
surged westward
toward the Golden Gate.
Standing at the bow
with the wind
in our faces,
you were pensive
and I remembered how
you often tell me
with a sigh and shake
of your head
that I am a dreamer
from another world,
but looking at you
then I knew
I am not
the only one.

On Your Birthday

When you are with me
my days are full.
You linger
in my mind
like salt breeze
and the smell
of new-mown grass
in summer,
sweet and fresh.
But time passes
too quickly
with our lives
pressed into
fleeting hours.
Let us go
more slowly, love,
and walk together
by the sea.
At least for now
it need not matter
that the world
careens around
if we hold fast
to what we have.

On Stinson Beach

Years from now
I will ask you
to walk on Stinson Beach
at dusk, where
footsteps kick
up dark sand
and the wind blows
shoreward, leaving
words lingering
in the evening light.
You will look
at me with
long-lashed eyes
with fine lines
at their corners,
and your hair
windblown
across your face,
understanding everything,
there in the Pacific twilight
with salt-spray
coming off the breakers,
at dusk on that
Stinson Beach
of my imagination.

Night Walk

When you walk again
on a clear night
and sense
the touch of stars
remember that
their soft light
arches over
another coast
where cities glow
across the Sound
with only wind to
break the silence
as I wonder
about the paths
we choose
and whether
the stars make
any difference.

Mnemosyne in 22 C

The starswept sea
glistens below
with only muted engines
and drifting clouds
to mark our passage.
I doze restlessly,
oblivious to
the coming day.
But desire
doesn't hold the night
any more than you,
falling farther behind
with each
passing moment.

The violet dawn
bathes the stars
in a tropic sea
and soon the light
explodes in red and coral.
Relentless engines
push us eastward
into morning.
People stir and wake
an hour out of Paris,
but I lag behind
near the edge
of night,
only Mnemosyne
my companion
somewhere between dawn
and the sinking moon.

Ephemera

We walked by the sea
on a March day
with salt haze
veiling the far shore
in lemon light.
You knelt by
the water's edge,
looking like a schoolgirl,
picking pebbles with
rose hues glowing
in the touch
of the receding tide.
But pebbles
lose their luster
as they dry,
leaving us
only words
to mark that
time by the sea
when the sky
arched over us
and seabirds called
our names.

Paper Butterflies

For you
    who make
the season bloom,

paper butterflies
        to banish gloom.

Fluttering
        beauty
    in the air,

            imagined garlands
for your hair.

. . . shoreward, toward home

Peonies

Yesterday I divided
the peony whose leaves
brush the house,
pressing the shovel
through the roots
until they yielded
to my weight
on the blade.
The new plant
faces east
where the morning
sun will warm it,
but first it must wait
for autumn's cold rain
slanting off the sea,
and for the winter fog
twisting through the inlet
to bead its barren stalks
with droplets
that seep to its roots
while I lie
in the fading darkness,
watching the channel
buoy light
and listening to
gull calls,
imagining crimson flowers
in a still-distant spring.

Tide Hole

West of Crane Neck
where boulders
from the bluff
fall into the sea,
waves at high tide
recede from the shore,
roil the surface
and twist the kelp
in the seawind.
Beach pebbles
catch the glow
of the winter sun,
their quartz and amethyst
holding cold fire
here where gulls
soar over their shadows
on the sand.

Virginia Garden

Roses and clematis
climb in the haze
and stillness
of late summer,
with soft afternoon light
brushing their foliage.
I sense the garden's subtlety,
and how the gardener
must have planned
its colors and textures,
marveling that
while I only write poems,
others can grow
metaphors.

Equinox

for Lisa Spinner

The lovers seem
small against
the sweep of sky
as sunlight slants
across the hillside
in early spring.
Her arm rests lightly
on his shoulder
and her brown hair
meanders beneath them
as they sense
the meadow's warmth
and the rhythms
of each other's hearts.

But the equinox
passes too quickly
and we all yield
to fate and seasons,
so dream that
the dandelions
that touch you
with their joyous cover
are galaxies
of nearby stars,
while for you each,
there is no other.

Laundry Ballet

This morning
I washed clothes
and hung them
on a line
between two oaks
behind the house
colored shirts
khaki pants
bright towels
brushing my face
smelling of soap
just clothes
until I saw them
move in the air
sleeves linked
pants pirouetting
in the wind
and sunlight
on this ordinary
day when I
washed clothes
and hung them
out to dance.

Semester's End

The squirrel
eats red berries
in the viburnum
near my window,
blending into
the grayness
of the campus
on the day before Christmas.
Soft shadows
fall across essays
stacked on my desk,
reminders of grading
I must finish soon.

When I look again,
the squirrel is gone.
In its place a starling
bobs its head,
spewing fragments
from its beak that
make bright red spots
on fallen leaves,
like the words
I write on papers
in the quiet room.

Washington Commuter

We fly north,
lulled by humming engines
and the sunlight
glinting from propellers
that curve into
spinning hubs.
Our shadow
crosses farms
locked in winter
until we leave
the land behind
and pass over
the open sea
where ship wakes
slice across swells.
Soon we dip toward
Fire Island,
banking steeply
over clam boats
working the bay
and startling
the gulls.
Hydraulic pumps whine,
the gear locks down,
and we bounce twice.
The trip is almost
over but I must
remember to stop
for bread.

Earthfall

Three miles up
clouds hold
the last rays
of tangerine sun.
Ocean swells glow
copper in the
fading light.
Neon Atlantic City
slides beneath us,
upstaged by twilight.

Over the Chesapeake,
with strobes flashing
like fireflies,
flaps down,
engines muted,
we descend to the rim
of a world
that does not
stop spinning
while I remember
beach roses on
the shore
by a distant sea.

Interlude

We sat by a stone wall
above the lake
in pale sunlight
by the budded sycamore,
sharing cold chicken,
bread, and a pear.
I read aloud
while you listened.

The sailboats
were white triangles
on the water.
I sensed the coming
spring, needing
nothing more
than our friendship
on that day
when the air
was filled
with dreams.

Currents

I remember how
you watched
on a summer day while
your grandsons pushed
the little boat and
scattered killifish.
When a breeze drew
the boat away
we swam and followed
until you caught it
off the bar,
bringing it back
to the children
who tugged
at your always
precariously draped shorts.

Now your grandsons
are men and you are borne
by a stronger current.
Again I follow
but can't hold you
against the unrelenting pull.
Yet in memory we press on
against an ebbing tide
as clouds shadow the sea.
There, as wind and current
ease, I touch you gently,
calling you shoreward,
toward home.

Laboratory Man

(for Miles Pickering)

You left us before
the end of class
taking your wit,
brogue, and quick pen
("Man against white space,"
you used to say)
leaving unread exams
and notebooks piled
on the stone tables
in the old laboratory.
Students who always
crowded around you
will ask for you this fall.
How can we explain?
Your lab coat still hangs
on the chair by the window
where sunlight caught
the chalk dust
in its brownian jig.
I suppose we must
pack your books
but we will leave
for September's freshmen
the echo of your laugh
carrying across rooms
where faded words
and numbers on dusty slates
mark your passage,
as if we could forget.

. . . no second chance

The Trial Counsel Rests

for Thomas J. Kennedy Jr., CAPT. USMC

Hey babe if you
were only here
we could
get together
now and then
to tell stories
and kid around
the way we did
long ago when we were
quick to compete
and even quicker
to laugh
with it all
ahead of us
but it didn't
work out
the way we thought
with promises unkept
and too many things
left undone
and now I can just
reach high enough
to run my fingers
slowly Jesus so slowly
over the gold letters
of your name
on the Wall.

Gift at Chorwon Valley

for Charles Sewell, LTCOL. USMC

I still wonder
what you thought
on the strafing run
'as stick-figures
on the ground
ran and hid
and you eased
the throttle
with your gloved hand
and rolled
into the turn
tracking through
the gunsight.

I wondered what made you
see them as men
stumbling in the mud
caught by the machine
and their bad luck
until you kicked in rudder
releasing the trigger
stopping the shells
long enough
for them to gain
the shelter of the trees.

You wondered later
what they were like
lying in the shadows
with their hearts racing
out of breath
pressing their faces
and sweat-stung eyes
against the earth
to which we all
must someday return,
but not that day
for them
or yet for me
remembering you.

July 1953

for Marshal McCook, CPL. USA

Jesus Christ Marshal
if I told
you once I told you
a thousand times
not to be
a hero
and to keep your
red head and wide
smile down low
while they talked
at Panmunjom
to end a forgotten war
so why did you
get yourself killed
wasted for no reason
just before
the truce
I need to understand
and I don't
please tell me
so I can explain
to your mother
she asked me
to look after you
God damn it Marshal
just tell me
why?

Evasion Course

Branches arch
across the road
in the pine forest
whose needles
muffle our footsteps.
The last traces
of light
touch on the
marsh to the east
where blue herons
stood last night
in the ebbing tide.

It is quiet now
and dusk
masks watchtowers
looming above
the meadow where
only warning signs
and empty cartridges
show that here
where wildflowers bloom
we hunt or elude
each other in ways
that have nothing
to do with love.

Accident Report

(for Steve Lapinsky, lstLT., USMC)

you were such
a hotshot pilot
how come you couldn't
keep from flying into
a mountain when you
knew I would miss your
clowning around
and spend much time
thinking how good
it always was
to have you with me
when things had
to go just right
the first time
no wave-offs
no second chance
but maybe just
this once
please.

remembering

flowers
growing only
in memory now
are as fragrant
as those that will
come again
in spring

Nuclear Negotiation

Today in Geneva
we sit in a room
where pale light
filters through curtains.
When our eyes meet
we quickly look away,
before choosing words
leaving nothing to chance
that tell of explosions
in Nevada and Kazakhstan
where instruments
measure earthtides
that rise and fall
adding new chords
to polyphonic
whale songs ringing
in cold seas.

Las Vegas casinos
shake but hookers
don't notice
while at Yucca Flat
Joshua trees
stand mute
and wild horses shy.
On Novaya Zemlya
bears turn their heads
to sniff the wind
lumbering onto
the Barents pack ice
while salmon race
through the strait
knowing more of mysteries
than we who wait
for zero-time
with pheromones
pulsing like those
of lovers stirred
by the soft scent
of as yet uncharred skin.

Unfinished Piece

for James Raz

You strong women
who marched
by Greenham Common
and in Kazakhstan
watched us
take the missiles
away and went home
but we saved
the warm plutonium
and explosive lenses
with arming circuits
choreographed to wait
intact until
they are needed
so you strong women
of Greenham Common
and Kazakhstan
don't give your
walking shoes
and signs away
just yet.

About the typeface:

This book is set in a typeface adapted from the work of the 16th century Paris publisher and designer Claude Garamond, whose sharply drawn characters were unsurpassed in his time for grace and beauty.